SIDE HUSTLE PASTOR

"How To Put Food On Your Table & Fund Your Ministry"

BY

MYRON PIERCE

Table of Contents

Foreword

At first glance, the term "side hustle" may not seem like much. Perhaps you've heard of the term used to describe a way to supplement your income, or as a hobby. Not a real business, just an activity that might net you some extra cash if you keep at it. You might be wondering, "Why start a side business? I'm a pastor, not an entrepreneur!"

Our culture is rapidly changing. Recent statistics from Giving USA and Tithe.ly, show giving to churches or religious organizations consist of only one-third of the $410 billion charitable giving in the United States. These stats show a downturn from the 1980s when giving to churches or religious organizations was fifty-seven percent.

What does all of this mean? Simply put, people are still giving, just not to churches. There is a hard reality that you and I need to accept. The days of massive capital campaigns to fund building projects, community outreach, missionary support, and so many other ministry pursuits are gone.

The considerable growth in the nonprofit sector, coupled with the availability of digital platforms, has made giving to social, environmental, and educational causes easier and more popular. Unfortunately, giving to churches is no longer at the top of the list for most people in America today.

As our society in the West continues to drift further into a Post-Christian culture, we, as ministers of the Gospel, will need to become both economic and social innovators. If we are going to reach the lost, plant churches and do the work that God, we must come up with creative solutions to generate capital and expand our efforts.

Rather than seeing this negatively, we should see this as an opportunity! It's not about creating the newest, flashiest tech startup but a way to provide for ourselves, our families, and our communities.

Social Enterprises are the way of the future. A social enterprise is the blending of a for-profit business strategy, with the mission and vision of a non-profit. The question for all of us is, "How can we fund our ministry with our current assets and skillset?

When my wife and I first started our small business, we had a lot of questions and didn't know where to turn to find answers. There was a lot that we didn't know. Today, I use my experience to coach business owners on how to strategize and launch their businesses in the marketplace. This experience has convinced me that we don't only need Google, Facebook, and our phones, but people in our lives that can help us see the best path forward.

In this book, Myron Pierce takes us on a journey of self-discovery. He is a Side Hustle Pastor, church planter, he develops leaders, and runs multiple businesses. Myron does this all while raising a growing family. He is a practitioner who's not afraid to take risks, make mistakes, and scale a ministry or a business from the ground up.

As you read *The Side Hustle Pastor,* I pray that you will begin to see how your giftings, skills, and experiences align with a need in the market and your community.

May you be encouraged that He who began a good work in your life will fulfill it, providing you with all that you need to walk according to his calling and purpose.

Logan Lee
Omaha, NE
November 2019

Introduction

Theology of Side Hustling

Thank you so much for taking the time to invest in your leadership as a side hustle pastor. Throughout this book, I will lay out a theology for having a side hustle. When we think about the landscape of Christianity in America, one of the affluent areas is the opportunity to do ministry full-time and fully fund a sustainable church. That's a top-level luxury for us in America, but things are changing in our culture. The trend shows Christianity is losing ground in America, and this will affect the funding ministry in the future. The reason I am writing this book is that it will be you and I, the side hustle pastors, who will chart a new way to do and fund ministry.

One of the things that I want to encourage you is to step into is the whole thought process behind being a side hustle pastor. Now, what's a side hustle pastor? A side hustle pastor is a man or woman who can fund their pocket and fund the powerful ministry that is happening in the local church. A side hustle pastor grows an enterprise that makes space for other people to be discipled. I want to explain to you the theology behind this because I want you to understand that my framework works and is legit.

One of the things I see in the Bible is the process of how the nation of Israel was freed from slavery. One of the things that stands out to me in this story in Exodus is how God positions Moses to be a leader of this movement. The obvious thing that helped Moses was his education. It was Moses' strength. He had grown up in an empire that had the privilege of an excellent education. Moses understood what it meant to be privileged. Privilege in terms of the Egyptians was a privileged population when compared to the Israelites. The Egyptians had power, opportunity, and wealth. When compared to the Israelites, the Egyptians had everything. Moses used that privilege as a platform to get training and education. Moses' thinking was beyond the average Hebrew slave when it came to school. Now, what that afforded Moses, was an opportunity to become a liberator, even though he second-guessed himself. Now, as Moses liberating and leading this liberation movement from Egypt to the Promised Land, God instructs the people. God says, "I want you to go knock on the doors of the Egyptians. I want you to go back to your enemy. I want you to go and raise money."

God also tells the people of Israel, "Hey, listen. I want you to knock on the doors of your enemy. I want you to go fundraise the project that we're about to undergo in your transition." At this moment, God turns the whole nation into side hustlers. They go back, they knock on the door of Israel, of the Egyptians, and then they ask them for money. They ask them for resources to build this project in the wilderness that we know as the tabernacle.

The Egyptians were favorably disposed towards the Israelites. Slaves are going to the door. Millions of them are going to the gates of the enemy, and they're raising money. It's easy because the favor of God is on these people. After all, God has a plan for them. I don't want you to miss that. God has a plan to build a local church. God has a plan to build a community of people who have an ethos whereby the spirit of God may dwell, liberate, free, build, and make disciples. So, what happens, this local fellowship becomes available because of the opportunity that they leveraged to go back to the very people that they were leaving.

How does this become a framework for our understanding of theology? Whenever God wants to build something, He co-operates and co-labors with you and me as His agents to fully enhance what He wants to do. When you think about building anything that God calls you to, it takes money. Often the money comes from inside and outside of the house. In this particular case, God uses an external donor to fund the project. A vital dynamic to notice between this external donor and the funded project is the people of God. I want you to capture this. If you are going to support the ministry and make sure there is food on your table, you, my friend, are the bridge.

You are the bridge to seeing this project happened. You are the bridge to seeing a community grow. The first thing that is highly important is we must begin to think about the vehicles that God will use to fund your ministries. The second thing that comes to my mind is the story of the Prophet Nehemiah. In the first chapter of the book, Nehemiah gets wind of the utter destruction of Jerusalem. The walls burned down, and his homeland is in disarray. Nehemiah begins the process of grief that morphs into prayer, which is then noticed by King Artaxerxes.

God, ultimately, uses Nehemiah as a leader. I'd suffice to say as an entrepreneurial leader. Upon seeing his anguish, the king asks Nehemiah, "Hey, what's going on? Something's different about you. Your countenance has changed." At that moment, Nehemiah begins casting vision for bringing restoration to his desolate homeland. As Nehemiah casts this vision, he also begins to lay out a strategy. During those moments, the king then gets behind him and says, "I'm on board." Now, this whole initiative is birthed out of Nehemiah being, primarily, a justice contractor.

Nehemiah wants to rebuild what has been broken and torn down. He wants to change the economic landscape of his community. Nehemiah wants to see the worship of God restored. He wants to see the people of

God back in place of God because, for them, Jerusalem was the city of God. It was the place of worship. It was the epicenter of all social and spiritual engagement. This side hustle leader captures a vision for his community and leverages the resources by being a contractor, mostly, to see this project fulfilled in 52 days. This story is where we find our framework for being a side hustle pastor. A couple of other people come to mind when I think about being a side hustle pastor.

Paul, the Apostle, was a Pharisee of Pharisees. Then Paul has an encounter with Jesus on the way to Damascus. After that, Paul begins planting churches all over and spends a couple of years as a tentmaker. Not as an employed tentmaker, but as a tentmaker who had his own business. For the Apostle Paul to pursue, this is pretty interesting. The reason Paul is important because we see that he is involved in both in full-time ministry and the marketplace. Paul and his team are going after the souls of men and women, and impacting the local economy, in tandem. Then we see the third element of Paul the Apostle as he's partnering with the local churches to raise funds to distribute to other churches. I don't want you to miss the fact that the Apostle Paul, and church leaders Priscilla and Aquila, are engaged in this side hustle that is allowing them to eat. We see it theologically in Paul's letters as he says, "If a man doesn't work, he can't eat."

Lastly, one of the things that I love is in the New Testament is found in the Book of Acts. In Acts, we see a man named Barnabas, who was a business leader, but he's also engaged in ministry. I love it because it tells me that you could be a side hustler. It tells me that you can have a level of leadership in the local church, and simultaneously engage the community, and put money on the table, funding the movement. That's what Barnabas did. In the book of Acts, it says: "He took some of the properties that he owned and sold them and came back and put it at the Apostle's feet."

That is the kind of leader that I'm talking about you and I becoming so that we can build a resourceful movement that helps to establish the work of God, as we see more people experience the goodness of God. I'd love for you to go back to the Bible and look at the story of the Exodus. Check out the story of Paul, Priscilla and Aquila, and Barnabas. Gather some conviction. Look at the revelation that God may provide you. Then begin asking yourself, what is it that I truly believe about this? Can it fit into my model of ministry? Can I make it work so that future generations might experience the blessing of knowing Jesus?

Chapter 1

Investing In You

Let's take some time to focus on growth, and what I mean by that, is your ability to grow as a side hustle pastor. The ability to understand how to generate revenue is dependent on your ability to invest in you. If you're just entertaining the idea of being a side hustle pastor, tells me a little bit about your capacity. It tells me that you can steward more than the average pastor.

You can function in two worlds. You can steward the serving of a market that needs something that you can supply. Also, you're able to lead the flock. That says something about your capacity. Let's not stop there, though. I want you to be able to increase your capacity. I want you to increase your investment in you because people are counting on you. I want to give you a couple of ways that you must invest in yourself. As an entrepreneurial leader, you must invest in yourself as a side hustle pastor. A lot of people want to cut corners on investing in themselves, and they want everything for free. As a side hustle pastor, you have to get your hands on all the freebies.

Whatever you're going after, whatever niche that you're going to insert yourself into, you have to find the freebies. Listen, bootstrapping your side hustle is essential. You're not trying to go into debt over this or have high operating costs, if at all possible. There are three places to start to keep the cost down: number one, Google, everything to learn. Second, YouTube it. Third, listen to podcasts. If you're interested in starting a side hustle and you have no previous knowledge, learn from other people's experiences. The great thing is the terms of engagement have changed regarding education, and these three platforms will help.

One of my companies is a digital marketing agency, so I am always looking to grow in the science of social media, social pros, and marketing school. To learn, I have invested in myself through engaging Google, Youtube, and podcasts. I continue to learn from these three platforms. One thing to do is for you to take copious notes. As you invest in yourself, you have to activate what you're learning. As you learn it, do it.

Another thing that I have learned is we are a product of the circles that we entertain. Show me your friends, and I'll show you your future. We've all heard that before. In the area of your niche, in the field of your market, in the area where you want to be side hustling, you need a 360 group:

- You need to find someone who is already there where you are trying to go into business.
- You need a 360 peer investment group. I don't mean financially. Someone besides me, we're in the same position when it comes to our process.
- Thirdly, someone under you. As you grow, you want to have the foresight of raising another side hustle pastor.

If you can find these three people, you are setting yourself up to be successful when it comes to getting a return on your investment.

Lastly, you invest in yourself by hanging out with professionals. This will cause you to spend some money. One of the guys that I'm learning from is Ty Lopez. This guy is a genius. He's more of a marketing guru, and he can sell you on anything. If you are considering developing a digital marketing agency, he is a great person to watch. Ty Lopez can teach you things for free, but I also pay my hard-earned money to learn from his guy. I have invested in his social media marketing agency training.

I love Ty Lopez's training because he lays it out for me. He helps me as a side hustle pastor get ahead. Ty Lopez is just one of many people that I would encourage you to learn from for your future. Who are people like Ty Lopes, icons, who's iconic in your niche? Whoever that maybe, you have to pay for what they know, just like you're paying for what I know. It's essential, and it's the way that we get to the next level. If you want to get to the next level, become the greatest, grandest, most impactful, side hustle pastor, you have to invest in you.

Chapter 2

Questions You Must Answer

There are five questions that you must answer when it comes to being a side hustle pastor. The number one question that we hear our kids ask us at the age of two is, you guessed it, "Why?" So, my question is: why do you want a side hustle? What's the motivation? If the motivation is, I want to make a lot of money. Then what happens in the first six weeks when you don't make a lot of money, or the first six months when you don't achieve the progress you were hoping to accomplish?

Why do I want a side hustle? One of the things that I think is very important to realize is, side hustling isn't for everybody, but it is for everybody. What are you calling in this season of ministry? I don't want to answer that for you, but it is t critical for you to know the answer to your "why." You and I both know that our "why" keeps us moving forward. Our "why" encourages us when we're down. Our "why" helps us cast vision to who we may be inviting into the ventures that we launch and establish. This question will help frame what you end up doing when it comes to side hustling.

The second question is, "What do I already know?" I mentioned in a previous chapter that if you don't know what you want to do, learn it from the pros. Realize that approach is It's going to take you longer, and that is great. If you desire to launch a side hustle fast and get moving forward, then one of the things you have to explore is: what do I already know?

When I lived in Colorado Springs and ran out of money a year and a half into a church plant. I had to ask myself the same question: what do I know how to do to make money?

When I was 16, my uncle gave me a job. His reason was to keep me off the streets and out of trouble. The role my Uncle gave me was car detailing, and I became great at it. What did I do in Colorado Springs when I ran out of money in my second church plant? I started a detailing company. The point I am trying to make is for you to look at what you already know how to do. When you look at your past experiences, you will find things you are a pro at, and that will help you. It will give you a sense of direction with your side hustle.

Another question that I think is important to starting a side hustle is, "what am I already good at?" If you miss that question, you could go down a road that wouldn't be healthy for you. My guess is you have experience in a specific field, from a placed you worked, or maybe you are naturally good at something. Maybe though life people have told you, "Man, you're good at that. Have you ever thought about starting a business?" These things are essential to pay attention to, because it may be the key to launching your side hustle.

The fourth question to explore is, "do I have a hobby that I can turn into a hustle?" For example, my wife and I are in ministry together. She's a side hustle church planter's wife, and she's very, very crafty. She has a gift box. Anytime people need a gift, she goes in that little gift box and grabs one out. I swear, it never runs dry. My wife is not only crafty, but she is also artistic and creative. With her passion for crafts and skills, she decided to launch a tee shirt business recently. Why? The answer is she was already doing crafts, like making earrings and small gifts for people, so she pivoted that into a t-shirt business. My wife decided to turn her hobby into a hustle. Our church is one of her contracts, and we go to her for tee shirts all the time.

If you have a hobby that you love to do, simply find a way to turn that into a side hustle. I guarantee you there is a demand for your hobby in the marketplace. Looking at your hobbies is an easy way to turn something you love to do into a hustle.

The fourth question you need to answer is: "what do I need to learn?" There are gaps in all of our learning. It is essential to find those gaps and start learning. If we can fill those gaps through learning it, we accelerate us into a great side hustle pastor. What are your weaknesses? For me, I was a consumer when it came to social media marketing, but I wasn't a side hustle pastor. There were things I needed to learn to become a business leader and not just a consumer, consuming Facebook.

Let me leave you with a bonus question because this question morphed our side hustle into a serious revenue-generating stream. The bonus question is, "can I team up with someone and start a side hustle?" That's the very thing that I did. Why? I knew that I didn't have the margin to run a full-fledged roofing business. What did I do? I partnered with my best friend, and we started a roofing company. Now I know you've heard, don't do a partnership with friends. The truth is people are lying. My friend and I are better together. Here is the key to how we make it work. Your vision, your mission, your core values, must be 80% the same. If they're not, don't do it.

Here's what I want you to do. Go back over those five questions plus the bonus question and begin to answer them.

Chapter 3

Startups You Can Start

In this chapter, I want to give you some quick and easy startup ideas that will onboard you into "side hustle pastoring." The first thing you can do right now is you can write a book. One time I went to the country of Georgia. While I was there, God spoke to me. God said, "I want you to write a book." I replied to Him, "Write a book?" He spoke again to me and said, "Yeah, I want you to write a book on rediscovering evangelism." In a week, I wrote a book. In thirty days, I published the book. My belief is you can do this as well! In the first book, I would recommend that you write your story. It's the most marketable. You have been through something, seen some things, and heard some things. Now you are transformed. The gospel is at the center of who you are, right? If you answered yes to any of those questions, you could write a book.

The second thing that you can do is start your own speaking business. I started speaking ten years ago when I got out of the penitentiary. I started speaking everywhere, and anywhere someone would have me. Now I'm speaking on larger platforms. I believe God is opening up more massive doors for me because I was faithful in speaking in the small. Many of you are speaking every Sunday already.

I want to encourage you to consider writing a book or invite you to begin launching your speaking business. Those are already in the lane of what you do as a pastor.

Number three. Go work for Uber, Lyft, Door Dash, taxi. Just pick one. One of the congregants in our church is making $800 a week. That is $800 a week. Let me say that again to make sure you get it. She's making $800 a week from driving. Working for one of those places is a cool and simple way to launch a side hustle. The great thing about it is you're the master of when you want to do it. It's convenient, so learn.

Another idea is teaching. Last year I taught at the college as an adjunct teacher, and it was great. It was a side hustle, right? I was able to take my expertise as a pastor and leader and invest it in the next generation. Guess what? They paid me to do it. My suggestion is that maybe you should start a business as an adjunct teacher. Find new places that will allow you to teach your craft.

The next idea is a T-shirt business. This is probably one of the coolest things that you can do. It doesn't take a lot of money to start up. First, visit the website, teespring.com. You can buy a domain name from GoDaddy. Then mask teespring.com with your domain name. Next, you find a graphic designer on upwork.com to design you something. Finally, get a T-shirt press for a hundred dollars, boom, you're in the game.

You could start a cleaning business. You could do this at night. Go to the dollar store and get a cleaner called Amazing for dollar. Go and buy a vacuum from Target for twenty-five dollars. Get some washcloths for ten dollars and a broom for five dollars. For less than a hundred dollars, you have a cleaning business!

Another idea is event planning. My assistant just launched her own event planning business. Guess why she started it? For three years, she was planning and running various events for our church. After three years of experience, she realizes, "Wow. I think I can launch my own event planning business." Guess what she's calling it? Joyful Event Planning. Is that cool or what!

The next idea you could do is to become a consultant. Now, this may be a little harder to break in to, but if you have influence, knowledge, or expertise in an area, leverage it. One thing I launched was my social media platform. I started doing referrals and booking clients. Starting off, you may need to start at $25 an hour. Realize, though, with more experience and opportunity, you can grow and scale what you charge people.

Listen, valuable content is worth it. Right now, I am sharing with you the things that I have learned as a side hustle pastor. I am putting it in written form and also as webinars. The reason is that I want to help and train people in an area of my expertise. People pay me for my content, and they will do the same for you. Consider what area you could provide training for people who need it. Then build the content, put it on a platform, market it, sell it, and scale it. You can do that, and it will take some time. However, it's worth it because people will benefit from it.

Let me give you two more ideas. One is an Amazon business. This is huge right now. Amazon is a colossal giant in the area of online advertising. I have a group of leaders who run this type of business, and some are making $25,000 a month. You will want to invest money in training. The cost is around $1,000-1,500 for training. I would recommend the training because with it this can be a very productive side hustle.

The other idea is to become a Secret shopper. My wife and I have done this in the past. We signed up with a company called BestMark. I'm not doing affiliate marketing for them, so you don't have to use my reference, but you can make some real money. You can make a couple hundred dollars a week being a secret shopper. You could even take it to the next level and be a secret shopper in another city. My friend Greg is a secret shopper. He travels all over the country, working with churches, and even he has a book. Being a secret shopper gives Greg the time and resources to have this type of influence.

Below is a list of Side Hustles you can start $0 - $100 bucks:

-Blogger

-Bookkeeping Service

-Booth Rental

-Build Rock Walls

-Caulking Subcontractor

-Chimney Sweep

-Cleaning Gutters

-Cleaning Service

-Club Promoter

-Consultant

-Contractor or Subcontractor

-Counseling Service

-Deck Building, Repair, Washing, or Staining

-Auto Detailing

-Dog Waste Cleanup

-Event Planner

-Furnace Filter Changing Service

-Gardening Services

-Gutter Cleaning

-Handyman

-House-sitting

-Landscaper

-Lawn Mowing

-Painting

-Personal trainer

-Pet Sitting

-Personal Shopper

-Translator

-Upholstery
-Web Designer
-Window Cleaning

Chapter 4
Building an Army of Side Hustlers

What if every single person inside of your community became a side hustler? That reality could enhance and create opportunities for people who were jobless or who were facing different problems. Many of those problems could be solved because you took your congregation to the next level. We are trying to do this right now in our community. Over the last year, we have started five or six businesses. We have provided incubators, training, and seminars to help facilitate this type of culture in our church. Here is how we did and a map for you to create the same culture.

Number one, you need to become a promoter. Ask people consistently, "Hey, what dreams do you have that are in your heart from God?" If you promote this type of engagement in your church, I promise you it will multiply into a myriad of things. You may find that God wants your church to have an impact outside its four walls. To build this culture, you have got to promote it. You have to talk about it. It has to be a line item in your budget. Build and provide a platform for side hustle heroes to emerge so that you can make a difference in your community.

The next thing you need to do is you need to train side hustle leaders in your church. "But, Myron, I am trying to train myself." That's fine, but what if you went through the training in this book with others? Yes, I am permitting you to use this training in your church for free, so use it as a training tool for other leaders!

Then partner with other entrepreneurial organizations that are already doing this in your community. Imagine going to an organization that's not faith-based as a pastor and saying, "I want to partner with you." That would blow their mind. Ask me if I did it. Yes, so find it and do it.

If you want to build this type of culture in your church, you have to celebrate it. Talk about it every time you have a chance. Use social media to highlight stories and people who are doing it. Get in front of your church and say, "Hey, God is doing amazing things at our church. We are reaching people for the sake of the gospel. We are making disciples. We are making an impact in our community, and entrepreneurs are emerging in our church. I want them to stand up so that we can publicly encourage them and celebrate them."

What you celebrate multiplies. What you acknowledge creates traction. I want to encourage you to raise up an army of side hustle leaders in your church because they are already there. They just need a senior leader to point them to the promised land. That promise is the dream that God put inside of them. Someone just needs to see it inside of them.

Chapter 5

Launching Your Startup

Throughout this chapter, I want to give you fifteen steps to starting a business. You will learn the nuts and bolts of starting any business. In the previous chapters, we covered important principles. This chapter will get into nitty-gritty to get you started.

The number one thing to do is grab an idea. Vision is everything. Where are you going? What's in your heart? At this point, hopefully, something is growing. If it's growing, take the next steps to spur more growth.

Here's the second step. Do your research. You have to find out if there is a market for your dream. Find out who your competitors are, what is the supply and the demand, and what it will cost. It is vital to do the whole market research. You can go on sba.gov to do this market research. You can also google market research and begin researching your area.

Third, you need to build a business plan. I am a fan of the one-page business plan. Now, if you want to do a more extensive business plan after the one-page business plan, go to sba.gov. Then create an account and fill out their business plan. The SBA site will help you develop an eight to ten-page plan.

The fourth step is the legal side. To start, simply go to www.irs.gov and fill out the paperwork. This will put your business in the federal database. After finishing this process, you will get an EIN number, which is your business's social security number. You can also go to the IRS website and simply search EIN and began the process. It will ask you for your name, social security number, and what type of business you want to start. I recommend you select an LLC type business. If it does not list the kind of business you want to start, then click "other" and type it into the form. In the end, it will ask you if you desire to receive your EIN digitally. Always click the digital, so you get a copy of your EIN number immediately. You can download it to your desktop.

You are not done yet. The fifth step is to register with the state. If you register with the feds and you do not register with the state, then you are going to be in trouble. To register your business, you need to create either an Article of Incorporation or a Certificate of Organization. Now, there are many business structures that you can use, but as stated earlier, I advocate for LLC. The LLC is the most straightforward structure, and you can do the paperwork quickly.

To fill out this paperwork, go to your state's Secretary of State website. Again, you will fill in you the similar information you used to fill out the federal paperwork. One difference is you have to give them a name for the registered agent. The registered agent is the name of a person that is responsible for making sure things are done quickly and adequately. Finally, go to the Department of Revenue website and create an account. This account gives a business the ability to pay taxes quarterly as the company makes money.

The sixth step is opening up a bank account for your business. All you need is the documentation from the fourth and fifth steps. Once you open the account, they will give you an account number. Now you have an account just for your business.

The majority of the steps above do not cost any money. The only cost will be when you incorporate it at the state level. Every state's fee is different but expect to pay around a hundred dollars to incorporate.

Number seven, you want an accounting platform. Now listen, an accounting platform is essential. I'm going to give you some steps later about the website and stuff, but you must pick a user-friendly platform. Listen, I would say this, use Wave. Wave Accounting. It has training on YouTube, but it's easy. I run my own books for all three of my companies. Very easy, it's very user-friendly. Create your Wave account, and then you connect that account with your bank account. At the end of tax season, run a report and hand it into your tax person. Very simple.

Now that the legal side is taken care of and you have a bank account. The eighth step is getting a payment platform. I recommend Square. I run all my businesses through the Square App. It is incredible because you can send invoices, send estimates, and track everything. All you have to do is create an account and connect your bank account to it. It is a great platform, and the set up is free. Square only takes a small percentage when you make money

The ninth items to take care of is your branding/design and logo. Every company has a specific brand. If you do not know a lot about branding, I will encourage you to look at color psychology. Simply google color psychology to start. Then determine the heart or ethos of your company is, and look at the type of color you want. After that, go to upwork.com or fiverr.com and find a graphics designer. Now, you may have a graphics person in your congregation. If you do, then try to get it for free.

Next is buying a domain name. Simply go to GoDaddy and find your business name. You may need to be creative with this part. I would encourage you to use a ".com." If you didn't find a ".com," I would encourage

".biz" or ".cc," but always try to go for ".com" first. If you are a digital company, ".io" is good as well.

After you have gotten your domain name, you need a website platform. What I love to use for websites is a platform called Wix. I love Wix because it is easy and user friendly. You do not have to be a coder to build a great website with Wix. The cool thing about Wix is you can create an account and build a website before you have to pay for it. Then you choose a template and make your site. I love templates because you can adjust them. Once you have finished changing the template, you can publish it. When you publish, Wix will ask if you want to upgrade. That is when you take the domain name that you have and connect it to the site. Wix will walk you through how to connect that domain name to the site. Then I would go to get a G Suite account with Google. You can do this on Wix when you upgrade it too. Wix will ask if you want an email, you will say yes. When you get your email from G Suite, it gives you a whole back office.

The eleventh step is social media. Do not start out creating multiple levels of social platforms. Pick the one platform best for you. Facebook is about community, Twitter is about news, Instagram is about fixtures, Snapchat is just a crazy thing, and YouTube is about videos. Once you pick the platform, take all your branding, and upload all your pictures. Let me give you a newsflash: If you want to create banners for your Facebook page, you can go to canva.com. If you need stock images for your social media or website, you go to pexels.com, it is free.

The twelfth step is e-mail marketing. You must have an e-mail marketing platform so that you can connect with your audience or customers. I recommend using Mailchimp. Mailchimp is straightforward, user-friendly, and free. Mailchimp allows you to create lists of your customers and create campaigns for emails. Mailchimp has premade templates, so you do not have to create your own. Mailchimp gives the ability to have a communication system for your customers.

Once you have your email marketing set up, proceed to step thirteen, which is prospecting. It is essential to know how you are going to reach customers. You can obtain customers through word of mouth or use upwork.com. Upwork.com gives you the ability to do data mining or data scarping for potential customers. All you need to do is tell them, "Hey, I need to find customers for (fill in your business market). I need names, numbers, emails, and addresses for customers." Upwork will send you all the information. Then voila, you have emails that you use for email marketing.

Now you can start selling. At first, just sell what you have. This is where marketing is so important. I have given you ways to do email marketing, but you must think of different ways to market. I have a social media marketing training that I highly advise you to take. The training is more about obtaining first-time guests, but it also translates to how you collect customers as well.

Finally, begin thinking about how you are going to scale the business. As your business grows, you have to start thinking about employees, possible self-contractors, and systems to help your business scale with growth.

In this chapter, I have given you fifteen steps to start your business. My hope is that you apply these steps and go farther. I want to see you go faster for the sake of the kingdom.

Chapter 6

Raising Capital

Here is the first key to raising money for your side hustle. Keep the cost as low as possible. I would recommend bootstrapping. To bootstrap, you need to look at what you already have. The best way to do this is to answer three questions. What do I have in my possession that I can use to start my business, who do I know, what can I borrow? Listen, you do not need a lot of money. What you need is a lot of strategies and innovation. If you can start a business with the things you have, then you will keep the cost low.

Now, the second key is organizing a vision plan that you can promote. If you have ever done a strategic plan, the project can get complicated quick. I would recommend a one-page document to keep things clear and easy to promote. The vision plan will communicate why you are doing what you are doing. Your plan will inform how you are doing it, how it solves the problem you are addressing, and how it connects to your ministry. I have learned that you have to marry what you are doing in the marketplace with the ministry so people can get behind it. For example, when I said, "Hey, we want to start a roofing company where we can hire people getting out the penitentiary."

Suddenly, there is a social component to what I am doing. I am not only making money, but I am helping people. It is not just social, but a biblical approach to helping change lives.

Also, do not underestimate your friends and family when it comes to raising money. First, simply make a list by asking: who are my friends and family that believe in me? Go to all of them and say, "Hey, this is what I'm doing. Do you want to get behind me?"

The truth is you do not need a lot of money to start a side hustle. You just need something to start. As your business grows, so does the money to fund the dream in your heart. Another possibility is looking for organizations in your city that give small microloans. If you are aching just to get started, go to cabbage.com. I had to borrow money from cabbage.com to purchase our first rental investment property. If you work on expanding your horizons, you will find ways to make money.

Another avenue is to start business networking. I joined my local business commerce, and many business people act as referrals. As you talk to friends, family, to the commerce, and people within your sphere, ask them, "Hey, who do you know who would love to get behind this?"

Let me give you a fourth idea. You can crowdsource your business through Crowdfunding, GoFundMe to raise capital. State that you are starting a business and state what you are going to do. You see it all the time on Shark Tank.

Let me give you one more possibility. You may find a venture capitalist for micro-businesses, who is in your city. Go after them. Get to know them. Share your vision and let them know what you're doing.

Appendix 1

Skills Survey

The Side Hustle Skills Survey is designed to help you determine what skills you have that will help you develop and launch a successful side hustle.

People Skills: Communication, Customer Service, Supervision, Managing Relationships, Public Relations, Being Professional
Sales: Marketing, Promotion, Networking
Strategy: Research, Pricing, Analysis, Negotiation, Purchasing
Production: Innovation, Creativity, Problem Solving
Operations: Follow Through, Being Organized, Multi-tasking, Accounting, Staffing, Logistics, Money Management

1. Circle the skills above that you already have.

2. Rank the top six business skills. If a skill is not on the list, include it.

3. Of the top six skills, what are the three skills you are best at?

4. Take your top three skills and write down examples of how you have used them in your life and ministry.

5. Out of the top three skills, what is the ONE skill you are best at? What is that your answer?

Appendix 2

Passion Canvas

Passion is the fuel that every side hustle pastor needs to go the distance. Take some time to answer these five questions and use them to build upon your side hustle journey.

Appendix 3

SWOT Analysis

Every future Side Hustle must be analyzed if it is going to be successful. The SWOT analysis will assist you in building a healthy side hustle foundation. After you complete the study, think through what your next steps are to build a profitable side hustle.

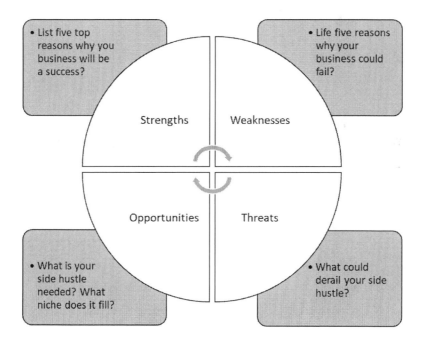

Appendix 4

Side Hustle Checklist

Business Name:
Business Address:
Business Owner(s)
Contact Phone #:
Contact Email:

BUSINESS

- What is the need for this business?
- Have you Googled the name and checked with your Secretary of State to see if it is available? If the name is available, register it with a Domain Registration Service like Go Daddy (Should cost about $ 10).
- Have you registered the business name with your Secretary of State? Do this as soon as possible, so no one else uses it? Why do you want to be in this business?
- Will you start this business from scratch, buy an existing business, or buy a franchise for this business?
- What licensing, training, or experience do you need for this? If more is needed, how can you get it?

- What is your work experience?
- What is your experience in this business, if any?
- Do you need to work for a company in this field before starting your own business, or can you learn as you go?
- What do you believe your strengths in this business will be?
- Do you have a specialty or a niche you can serve, if so, what?
- Who is your competition?
- Where are they located?
- What does your competition do well?
- What does your competition do poorly?
- What will make you unique or better than the competition?
- What is your "elevator speech?"
- Have you made a map of your city, which includes the location of your competition plus the place of any businesses that can be a positive or negative influence for you?
- Is the market underserved or saturated? Why do you think that?
- What is the target geographical area you will start serving? Expand to?
- What are the geographic limits of your service territory?
- What is your mission with this business, other than making money?

- Do you have anyone who can mentor you in your new venture?
- Who are your vendors and suppliers?
- What will you need to do to establish credit with them, and under what terms?
- What is your plan for the first 3 months?
- What is your plan for the first year?
- What is your plan for the second year?

CUSTOMERS

- Who are your target customers? Why did you choose this group?
- How will you relate to or be relevant to this group?
- What are the demographics of your target customer? Are they above, below, or at the average for your target geographic area?
- How will you reach your customers?
- How much will you spend on your initial advertising and promotions?
- How will you advertise and promote your business?
- Will you, or how will you, use "social media?".
- Do you know what the expected response rate of your proposed advertising?
- What is your competition doing to advertise and promote?
- Will you offer a coupon, special, or other promotion? If so, what?

PRODUCTS & SERVICES

- What is the cost and price of your product(s) or service(s)?
- How did you determine the cost and price?
- What is your starting inventory of the product, if any?
- How does your product mix, inventory, and proposed prices compare with your competition?
- Do you need any licenses or permits to work in an area?
- Do you need to collect sales tax on your goods and services?
- Do you need a logo? Do you need a website? Who will do your website if you have one? Will you make sales over the internet? Who will process your payments? Will you do your own order fulfillment, if any?

ADMINISTRATIVE, STAFFING, OWNERSHIP

- When/where can you get business cards? Where will you do your banking? Why?
- Do you need to accept credit cards? If so, who will you use? How many employees do you need? How much will you pay them?

47

- What are the job positions, and how many of each do you need to fill to function?
- How do you intend to operate the business?
- Is it just you, or will you hire managers? Do you have family members to help out?
- How will you train and supervise your team?
- Will you use subcontractors, if so, where and how?
- Can you operate your business from home, or do you need to rent a shop, store, or office space?
- How much space do you need for your business?
- Do you have an excellent commercial real estate agent to help you? Do you need to maintain a service department? If so, what do you need for facilities, equipment, staff, and supplies to operate it?
- What are you doing to provide customer service?
- How will it be owned? Will you incorporate, make an LLC (limited liability company), or a partnership?
- Who all will own the business (list percentages, ownership and responsibilities of any partners)
- If it is a corporation, who are the officers?

FURNITURE, FIXTURES, & EQUIPMENT (FF&E)

- What equipment, tools, computers, vehicles, and furniture do you need to have?
- *W*here can you buy them?
- Can you buy them used for less than new? What will each item cost? Is there a monthly payment associated with them?
- How will you pay for them? (loan, personal funds, money from a partner, or investor)
- Will you lease or rent them? Can you get these items on a payment plan, or with delayed payment, and pay for them from the operation of your new business?

INSURANCE and LEGAL

- How much will your insurance cost?
- Who is your insurance company, and what is the policy number?
- Do you have an attorney? (*Name / P*hone Numb*er / Emai*l)

FINANCIAL

- Tax ID #: (www.irs.gov has these fo*r fr*ee. Se*ar*ch "E*mplo*y*er ID nu*mbers." *The*y *als*o have *links* to each State Ta*x ID #s*)

- Do you have a CPA or bookkeeper? (*Name / Phone Number / Email*) Who will maintain your financial records? *(Name / Phone Number / Email)* Who will handle your finances? (Na*me / Phone Number / Email*) What are your start-up costs? What can you do to raise money, if needed? Do you have friends, family, a bank, or an investor you can approach? How much have you budgeted for a start-up?

ESTIMATED START-UP LIST

- Payroll
- Contract labor
- Rent
- Utilities
- Internet
- Cell phones and telephones
- Website
- Insurance
- Bonding costs
- Banking expense
- Bookkeeping expense
- Vehicle expense
- Payroll taxes
- Income taxes
- Debt service and/or lease payments
- Supplies
- Materials
- Inventory
- Repairs
- Shipping

- Commissions
- Marketing
- Collection loss
- Legal/professional fees
- Franchise fees or license fees
- Savings and reserves

Appendix 5

One Page Business Plan

OVERVIEW

- What will you sell?
- Who will buy it?
- How will your business help people?

HUSTLING

- How will your customers learn about your business?
- How can you encourage referrals?

KA-CHING

- What will you charge?
- How will you get paid?
- How else will you make money from this project?

SUCCESS
- The project will be successful when it achieves these metrics:
  o Number of customers
  o Annual net income

OBSTACLES | CHALLENGES | OPEN QUESTIONS
- Specific concern or question #1
- A proposed solution to concern #1

WORKS CITED

Pelshaw, R.L. Illegal to Legal: Business Success for the (formerly) incarcerated. Pelshaw Group, 2017 Print.

SIDE HUSTLE Page 26-27   Below is a list of Side Hustles you can start $0 - $1000 *

from *Illegal to Legal: Business Success for the (Formerly) Incarcerated, pp 43,* © *2014 Pelshaw Group Inc. Used with permission www.pelshaw.com*

SIDE HUSTLE Page 42 Side Hustle Survey

adapted from *Illegal to Legal: Business Success for the (Formerly) Incarcerated, pp 18-19,* © *2014 Pelshaw Group Inc. Used with permission www.pelshaw.com*

SIDE HUSTLE Page 46-53 Side Hustle Checklist
(Based on the Business Plan Checklist™ from *"Illegal to Legal"*
www.pelshaw.com)

from *Illegal to Legal: Business Success for the (Formerly) Incarcerated, pp 18-19,* © *2014 Pelshaw Group Inc. Used with permission www.pelshaw.com*

Made in the USA
Monee, IL
06 February 2021